Thirty-Two Gates of Wisdom

AWAKENING THROUGH KABBALAH

Rabbi DovBer Pinson

Ben Yehuda Press

Teaneck, New Jersey

Published by Ben Yehuda Press
430 Kensington Road
Teaneck, NJ 07666

http://www.BenYehudaPress.com

Ben Yehuda Press books may be purchased for educational, business or sales promotional use. For information, please contact:
Special Markets, Ben Yehuda Press,
430 Kensington Road, Teaneck, NJ 07666.
markets@BenYehudaPress.com.

pb ISBN   1-934730-24-6
pb ISBN13 978-1-934730-24-9

Library of Congress Cataloging-in-Publication Data

Pinson, DovBer, 1971-
  Thirty-two gates of wisdom : awakening through Kabbalah / DovBer Pinson.
    p. cm.
  ISBN 978-1-934730-24-9 (pb)
  1. Cabala. 2. Self-actualization (Psychology)—Religious aspects—Judaism. I. Title.

BM525.P54 2008
296.1'6—dc22

                                 2008049696

08 09 10 / 10 9 8 7 6 5 4 3 2 1

DEDICATION

In gratitude to Tree of Life Foundation

To
Michael & Barri Shane
Rebecca, Emily and Tucker

With Abundant Blessings for Material and Spiritual Success
and True Nachas From Your Wonderful Children

Thank You

To my dear student Mattisyhu Brown for his effort with this text.
May he and his family be blessed. And may he rise higher and deeper in Avodas Hashem, and do so from a place of joy and expansiveness.

To all my students at the IYYUN Yeshiva and the IYYUN Center.

Many thanks to Mrs. Sherri Venokur for all her help.
May her support of Torah be a source of blessings to her and her entire family.

Contents

TORAH

PERSONA

NAME

QUALITY

ELEMENT

SOUL

Although all five worlds and beyond are present in Asiyah, most of us are not conscious of higher worlds.

Still, our actions can elevate fallen sparks, opening a flow from 'A"K' into the vessel of Asiyah

© Rav DovBer Pinson, Iyun Inc.

Torah (outer ring):

SOD SH'B'SOD — secret within a secret — of Torah & 613 Mitzvos
SOD — secret — of Torah & 613 Mitzvos
DERUSH — homiletical — of Torah & 613 Mitzvos
REMEZ — allegorical — of Torah & 613 Mitzvos
P'SHAT — literal — of Torah & 613 Mitzvos

Persona:

ARICH — Keser
ABBA — Chochmah
IMA — Binah
Z"A — Middos
NUKVAH — Malchus

Name:

Beyond all names, numbers, including all names, numbers
SHEIM A"V (72)
SHEIM SA"G (63)
SHEIM MA"H (45)
SHEIM BA"N (52)

The 10 Personal Character Traits

GEVURAH
TIFERES
NETZACH
HOD
YESOD
MALCHUS

Quality:

Beyond all names, numbers, including all names, numbers
PURE POTENTIALITY — beyond 'goodness'/negativity, polarity
TOV — Divine Goodness
RAV TOV / MIYUT RAH — more goodness than negativity
MECHTZA-MECHTZA — equal good and negative
RAV RAH/MIYUT TOV — more negativity than goodness

Element:

YULI — Ether
AISH — Fire
RUACH — Wind
MAYIM — Water
AFAR — Earth, Dust

Soul:

YECHIDAH — Transcendental 'Self' (transcend being)
CHAYAH — Spiritual 'Self' (be)
NESHAMA — Mental 'Self' (know)
RUACH — Emotional 'Self' (feel)
NEFESH — Physical 'Self' (act)

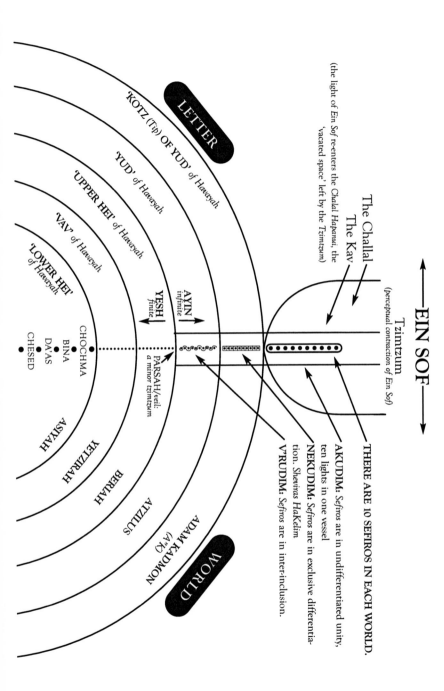

A MAP OF HISHTALSHELUS · THE GREAT CHAIN OF BEING

⟵ **EIN SOF** ⟶

Tzimtzum
(perceptual contraction of Ein Sof)

The Challah
The Kav

(the light of Ein Sof re-enters the Chalal Hapanui, the 'vacated space' left by the Tzimtzum)

LETTER

'KOTZ (Tip) OF YUD' *of Havayah*

'YUD' *of Havayah*

'UPPER HEI' *of Havayah*

'VAV' *of Havayah*

'LOWER HEI' *of Havayah*

AYIN *infinite* ⟶
⟵ **YESH** *finite*

PARSAH/*veil: a minor tzimtzum*

CHOCHMA
BINA
DA'AS
CHESED

ATZILUS
BERIAH
YETZIRAH
ASIYAH

ADAM KADMON *(A"K)*

WORLD

THERE ARE 10 SEFIROS IN EACH WORLD.

AKUDIM: *Sefiros are in undifferentiated unity, ten lights in one vessel*

NEKUDIM: *Sefiros are in exclusive differentiation. Sheviras HaKelim*

V'RUDIM: *Sefiros are in inter-inclusion.*

Thirty-Two Gates
of Wisdom

An Introduction

The Meaning of Kabbalah

Simply translated, *kabbalah* means "that which is received." This reflects the history of *kabbalah* as an oral transmission from teacher to student.

Looking deeper, the word *kabbalah* can mean to be open and receptive, to challenge one's own internal navigational system in order to see, hear, and be open to... more.

To fully absorb a teaching we must be receptive to it. We turn ourselves into vessels and invite within that which we wish to understand or grasp. In this way, we become receptacles, dispensaries and a part of the *kabbalah*.

We become vessels of this tradition by opening the self to a higher reality, and viewing the spirit within the matter. We raise our consciousness to the point where our perception of reality is altered and the Divine within all creation is revealed. As we pursue a deeper awareness, we become less ego-centered and more attuned to the deeper significance of our surroundings.

Four Varieties

Broadly speaking, there are four categories of *kabbalah*: Theoretical, Meditative, Magical and Personal.

The Theoretical approach concerns itself primarily with the inner dimensions of reality, such as spiritual realms, souls, and angels.

The Meditative method is utilized to reach elevated states of consciousness—even a state of prophecy—through the use of divine names and letter permutations.

The Magical path concerns itself with altering and influencing the course of nature. Its practice includes the use of divine names, incantations, amulets, magical seals and various other mystical exercises.

The Personal technique seeks to turn everything inward. The adept applies the wisdom to facilitate spiritual development and advancement, literally bringing heaven down to earth.

The History of Theoretical Kabbalah

The vast majority of *kabbalah* teachings that have been (and continue to be) revealed lie within the domain of the theoretical. At the heart of this type of *kabbalah* is the sacred work of the Zohar, The Book of Illumination, which consists of teachings of the 2nd century Talmudic mystic, Rabbi Shimon Bar Yochai. These teachings were handed down from one generation to the next until they were published in the late 13th century by the Kabbalist R. Moshe De Leon.

Full appreciation of the Zohar's wisdom was attained in the 16th century by the mystics of Safed, Israel. This particular period in history is referred to as the great Kabbalistic renaissance. The Safed movement was steered by the profound and systematic teachings of R. Moshe Cordovero, known as the Ramak (1522-1570), and particularly by the teachings of R.Yitzchak Luria, (1534-1572) known as the Ari-Zal, the Godly Rabbi Yitzchak of Blessed Memory.

Meditative Kabbalah

Meditative *kabbalah* was not popular during the Middle Ages. The greatest proponents of this method was R. Abraham Abulafia (1240-1296), who headed a mystical school primarily interested in reaching expansive meditative states.

R. Abulafia taught that prophetic insight could be attained through meditation. He used writing as a medium, writing the letters of a word over and over again in various styles and configurations. This repetitive exercise combines and separates the letters, composing entirely new motifs of letters—essentially playing the letters as music. Another more advanced method suggested the use of breath and the recitation of divine names while moving the head in the direction of the Hebrew vowels.

His teachings were attacked throughout his life, but years later they gained favor with the mystics of Safed.

Magical Kabbalah

The vast majority of the most important texts of magical *kabbalah* have never been published, and perhaps for good reason.

Many early Kabbalists consider magical *kabbalah* to be a dangerous discipline. Legend tells of R. Joseph Della Reina (1418–1472), one of the great masters of magical *kabbalah*, who attempted, along with some students, to use these magical techniques to bring about world redemption. Some say that his failure led to his suicide; others say he became an apostate. Still others say he simply went mad.

Kabbalists in the generations that followed understood his story as a warning against practicing magical *kabbalah*. From then on, the magical elements of *kabbalah* have, for all intents and purposes, become extinct, and their knowledge and practice have been completely forgotten.

Personal Kabbalah

This form of *kabbalah* takes all the theoretical and abstract teachings and the meditative and contemplative practices and turns them into an internal process, focusing on psychological and physical applications.

Having benefitted from the great teachers of *kabbalah* who came before him, R. Yisrael Ben Eliezer, (1698-1760), known as the Baal Shem Tov, ("Master of the Good Name"), developed these teachings even further. The Baal Shem Tov founded the Chassidic movement, which has continued to steer, inspire, and influence all other Kabbalistic movements until the present day.

The purpose of Kabbalah: coming full circle

Kabbalah's purpose is often misunderstood. A popular misconception is that the study of *kabbalah* results in one's transformation into a psychic, or perhaps a clairvoyant, capable of miraculous and otherworldly abilities. In truth, the purpose in the practice of *kabbalah* is to perfect the self. *Kabbalah* offers a means of becoming a more expanded, transcendent individual, attuned to the essence of one's deepest self.

An authentic and deep journey will come full circle and will return the practitioner to the world of the here-and-now. The Talmud tells of four sages who entered the mystical orchard (Pardes) and experienced a transcendental experience. Ben Azzai "gazed and died." Ben Zoma "gazed and was stricken," with insanity. Elisha Ben Avuyah "gazed and cut off his plantings," that is, became a heretic. Rabbi Akiva "entered and exited in peace."

The orchard represents the higher spiritual realms. Rabbi Akiva was the only one amongst these great sages who was able to enter and exit the mystical orchard without being scarred. A true, well balanced master, he realized that the objective was not to over-identify with the light and fail to return—physically, as Ben Azzai did, or mentally, as Ben Zoma did. Nor, was it to feel personal release or ecstasy, as Acher intended. Rather, the goal was to explore and return with the proper wisdom to serve in the here-and-now. Rabbi Akiva "entered" and thus "exited," whole and "in peace."

Ultimately, the purpose of our outward journey is to bring

back expansive new awareness to plant within our consciousness.

Let us open ourselves for the journey...

GATE I

Etzem – Anochi
'I'

Fire and smoke poured from the mountain and the earth shook. The entire Community of Israel stood together in awe at the foot of Sinai as the Divine Presence thrust them into profound revelation. The thunder of awakening surged through each heart and mind as a transcendent voice spoke out: "*Anochi HaShem Elokecha.*" The literal translation of this thunder is, "I am The Name, your G-d."

Where the people of Israel received this realization in an explosive flash, we can receive this truth gradually by unpacking and contemplating the mystic teachings in these three words:

♣ *Anochi* is the Divine 'I', a description of the Divine Self.

♣ *Hashem,* literally, "The Name," refers to God's attribute of Infinity that is 'beyond' and transcendent.

♣ *Elokecha,* (also called *Elokim,*) is a plural term, referring to the Divinity that interfaces with the finite world of multiplicity: meaning, "your personal G-d."

The limited human ego ("I") is called *ani*—composed of the Hebrew letters *aleph, nun,* and *yud.* When these letters are rearranged to *aleph, yud, nun* they spell *ayin,* "nothing," or emptiness. We refer to the Infinite as *ayin* because from the finite perspective, Infinity is intangible, it is no-thing, empty of "things." Conversely, from the perspective of the Infinite, the finite is nothing—the ego does not exist. The Infinite and finite are thus in perpetual tension and conflict.

The word *anochi*, referring to the Divine "I," consists of the word *ani*, plus the letter *kuf*—symbolic of word *Keter* meaning the Crown, the Ultimate. When the letters of *anochi* are rearranged, they spell *k'ani*, meaning "like an *ani*" or, "like an 'I'."

Anochi, the Ultimate "I," is like the ego 'I'. The Ultimate "I" is not elided with our personal self although it is very much a part of us. "*Anochi*" invites us to extend the metaphor of "personal self" to its fullest expression as a part of the Ultimate Divine Self.

Anochi is a synonym for *etzem* or *atzmus*, meaning "Essence"— the ultimate context and totality of Reality. Essence is no-thing and every-thing, and yet it is neither nothing nor everything. Descriptive terms such as these do not apply to *atzmus* because any adjective, even "infinite," is by definition a limitation.

Although Essence is beyond the finite and the Infinite, it embraces them both. For this reason, Essence holds the key to resolving the existential tension between the finite and the Infinite.

The "I" of *anochi* is the "I" of existence, the "I" of form, the "I" of thing, and the "I" of no-thing, the "I" of finitude and the "I" of infinitude, the "I" of fullness and the "I" of emptiness.

As the ancients received the revelation of *Anochi*, they encountered the unlimited Divine in the absence of conflict with their limited human existence. In this revelation, there was no duality, only One-ness. Essence cannot be "experienced," because nothing exists outside of Essence. Self-consciousness distances the mind from the experience itself.

Together, Every-thing and No-thing become a metaphor for Essence: Essence alone is not a metaphor. Every gate is a gate to Essence, and every practice is a practice of Essence. Yet, there are no gates or practices to *reach* Essence.

♣We cannot become that which we already are. The process may be simply a matter of revelation.

GATE 2

Ohr Ein Sof
The Endless Light

There is no way to relate to Essence, for we are *of* Essence. There is nothing outside of Essence, nor any division within it. Relationship suggests duality; essence is singularity. What begins with essence ends with essence, and there are no-things in between to obstruct that singularity.

Yet—and this is the supreme mystery—we are relational beings. Our brains are built to project definitions and distinctions, to compartmentalize and contextualize, and to relate to apparent separations as if they actually exist. Binary oppositions dominate our perception in our daily practices. This is like being awake, yet day-dreaming that we are asleep.

Our brains are hard-wired to break life into projects. Our consciousness is an instrument created to negotiate a three dimensional universe, which encompasses definitions. Without the ability to make distinctions, the mind has a hard time grasping what we call reality. Because of this, we feel separated from our Essential Source. The yearning to awaken to our Source is the fuel behind everything we do.

The kabbalistic ladder of metaphors, worlds, gates, and practices is the path to our gradual awakening to our true state: Unity.

The highest gate, the ultimate metaphor for Reality, is *ein sof*, 'No End'—Infinity. The *ohr ein sof*—Light of Infinity—metaphorically shines within Essence like a beginningless, endless light within the orb of a boundless sun.

Within the orb of the *ohr ein sof* there is no shadow, color, or limitation. There is nothing to bind the infinite light. In *ein sof* anything with even the semblance of a *sof*, an 'end', is *ein*, 'not.' *Ein* means *ayin*—absolutely no-thing. In Hebrew *ayin* and *ein* are spelled the same.

In personal terms: When we are fully engaged in expressing our endless selves, there is no room for a relationship with others. Relationships can only exist with boundaries. Without boundaries, our light would pour forth, leaving no room for anyone else.

❧ To enter the gate of *ein sof* is to become One with the Infinite Divine Light. All we need do is stay true to what we subconsciously already know: I am no-thing. I am not an independent, separate I and the *ein sof* is within Everything.

GATE 3

Tzimtzum – Contraction

An apparent paradox exists: the *ohr ein sof* is infinite and beyond form, yet the world we observe is comprised of *things* and multiplicity, beginnings and endings.

The 15th century kabbalists pondered this mystery and revealed the idea of *tzimtzum*: contraction and concealment.

In the world that presents itself to our senses, we observe countless transformations. One thing becomes another. When our physical bodies die, they become the soil which nourishes new life. Mineral feeds plant, plant feeds animal, animal feeds man, and man returns his minerals to the earth. Naturally, we tend to view the structure of creation as fluid and constantly evolving.

Using the knowledge that our eyes have taught us, we expect the *ohr ein sof* to emerge into *sof*. We anticipate that pure spirit, "Light," will eventually come to its end and transform into matter. But this is not so simple, for spirit cannot become anything other than spirit.

To understand how the *ohr ein sof* manifests within the *sof*, one can think of it in terms of *tzimtzum*. Instead of seeing the creation process as an evolution from unity to multiplicity, creation is understood in terms of a 'quantum leap' from oneness to multiplicity. The *tzimtzum*, the primordial contraction within Divine oneness, allowed an island of emptiness from which our universe emerged. The contraction of the Divine Self makes it possibility for finitude to exist within the context of Infinity.

In terms of human relationships: To fully sense the other, we need to become still.

❧ When we are less expressive of what we want, and how we feel, we become open to experience what the other feels and the other wants.

It is through such an act of *tzimtzum* that the Infinite allows the finite to simultaneously and overtly exist.

GATE 4
Igul - Circle

To create otherness and apparent separation there was the *tzimtzum,* contraction, of the *ohr ein sof* within itself and the contraction created a *chalal*—an empty, round space.

The displaced 'infinite light' encircled the empty space in the shape of an *igul,* circle. A circle holds no distinctions. It is a perfect shape in which any piece is the same as any other piece. In this place all potential reality was contained, without distinctions, without beginning or end.

The *igul* is like the seed which will eventually be articulated into a full blossomed and articulated tree. As the full tree exists undifferentiated within the seed, so, too, the *igul* is one seamless whole.

After the initial contraction, the infinite light was put aside and the finite began to emerge. The first thing to manifest was the potential for everything physical. A thin ray of straight light, referred to as the *kav,* beamed into the *chalal.* The *kav* immediately began to illuminate the perimeter of the *chalal,* forming concentric circles of light.

The human female embodies the *igul* shape and the *sefira* of *malchus* (which will be explained in Gate 14). The circle of the womb cradles both the female and male. The *kav,* or line, is embodied in the male form. His procreative organ represents the *sefira* of *Yesod* and contains traces of both line and circle, as the *atarah,* the corona, is the 'female' aspect within the male body.

In our own creative process, before we work out the details of how we are going to create—the line reality—we first have a general awareness of what we wish to create—the circle reality.

Overall, the previous three Gates reflect our own three stages of creativity. In the first stage we are pre-*tzimtzum*, we are enthused with an idea to create, for example, a novel or a painting, and we are brimming with excitement and exuberance. Step two is actually to sit down with pen or brush, and practice the discipline of *tzimtzum* by putting the inspiration to paper or canvas. As we begin to write or paint, the storyline or image is still in a state of circle, meaning that the creation has not yet been completely formulated and there are still multiple possibilities of what the creation ultimately will become.

❧ As we humans begin our creative enterprise, we begin with the inspiration to create—our *igul*. It is then up to a later stage in creativity, the *yashar,* to guide us with the 'how.'

GATE 5

Yashar - Line

The *ohr ein sof,* the endless light, went through a process of *tzimtzum*—the contraction which created an empty space. The infinite light encompassed the empty space, forming a circle. Then a line intruded—the idea of *yashar*—linear progression, where distinctions and the notion of "higher" and "lower" begins.

Where *igul* signifies possibility, *yashar* signifies actual reality (the former a more *kelalis,* general, yet causal condition, the latter a more *peratis,* specific, yet acausal condition).

The world of *yashar* has distinct points, and an up-and-down sequential structure, with a clear beginning and a definite end. The points along the *yashar* are the *sefiros.*

From our perspective, the head of the line appears closest to the Source of emanation. We observe the lower levels to be furthest from the Source of emanation. Yet, conversely from a perspective of "purpose," the lower is in fact higher, as the purpose is in the lower. In the *igul* circle image, however, the inner circles are lower and surrounded by the outer, higher circles.

♣ Our own creative processes begin with a general image of our creation.

We begin the slow process of implementation by following the path that makes itself apparent to us and working forward in a linear fashion.

GATE 6

Reshimu - Imprint

Everything we encounter leaves its mark upon us. Upon contact with something, it impresses upon us and we impress upon it, whether it is the people we meet or the objects we observe. On the quantum level, the observer alters the observed. On the human level, the independent 'I' of selfhood is an accumulation of all our experiences and all the people we encounter.

This truth is a microcosmic reflection of the macrocosmic creative process. Initially, there was only the *ohr ein sof*—the infinite endless light. After *tzimtzum* produced the void, *chalal,*, an imprint of the infinite light still remained within the empty space. Because *tzimtzum* by definition includes an encounter with the *ohr ein sof*, a *reshimu* of the *ohr ein sof* is imprinted within the void created by the *tzimtzum*.

Reshimu lo nogah ba ha'tzimtzum—the *tzimtzum* did not disturb the *reshimu*. Within the empty space of our finite reality, there remains a residue of the infinite transcendent light. Because every action leaves a residue, the power of positive action can tap into the infinite and thereby extend both forward and backwards in time. Through the process of deep transformation, *teshuvah*, this enables us to influence not only the present, but the past as well.

Connecting to the *reshimu*, our present actions can affect the past, and re-contextualize the trajectory of a negative past into something positive.

♣Our creative process can mirror the cosmic process. If we wish to actualize our creativity, we need the initial vision, the discipline to stick with it, and the ability to re-connect to the source of our inspiration. This re-experience of our initial passion to create is the imprint of our pre-*tzimtzum* inspiration.

GATE 7

Sheviras Hakelim
Breaking of the Vessels

After the initial retraction of the infinite light, the *tzimtzum ha'rishon*, the first contraction, where the finite came into focus, there was a *chazor ve'hier*—a return and illumination. The *ohr ein sof* shone once again, reopening the floodlights, this time shining through the prism of finite vessels which came into being after *tzimtzum*. These vessels are the ten points along the line. They are the *sefiros*. Once finitude was established, the *ohr ein sof* resumed illumination, and the vessels still retained their existence, albeit in the first process for a 'short time.'

Visualize sitting amongst people who are having a conversation that seems completely over your head. Until you open your mouth you feel overshadowed. Yet, the moment you say something, and assert even the slightest measure of presence, you no longer feel left out, even when the conversation resumes. The same is true for the "vessels" and the "infinite light"—once the vessels become manifest they maintain their existence, even after the "light" shines again.

The ten points along the length of the *kav* form a progressive hierarchy, the ten *sefiros*. For now let's imagine the *ohr ein sof* as colorless pure undifferentiated water and the *sefiros* as colored containers which hold the water.

Although the light itself is formless, endless and undiluted, by the time the *ohr ein sof* comes to the vessels after the *tzimtzum* the light is less intense. The further removed the vessel appears from the light the more dense and colored it will become; the light shining through it seems ever more dimmer.

The *ein sof's* light never changes. It is only through viewing the light passing through the distinct vessels that one light seems transparent and pure, one seems white and warming, and one seems dark blue and ominous. Now the Formless has assumed form; reflecting the attributes of the vessels: a loving, kind, strong or compassionate G-d.

On this level the *sefiros* are referred to as *nekudim*—dots, indicating that there was no coherence to them. Each one was unrelated to the next. Because of this lack of unity, the vessels (that is the lower eight vessels) collapsed and broke, overwhelmed by the *ohr ein sof*. This is the cosmic *breaking of the vessels*.

Although the infinite light shattered the finite vessels, traces of the infinite remained with the broken vessel shards. This is like pouring boiling hot water into a slim glass causing it to shatter. The pieces retain the heat of the water for a short period of time.

These broken vessels, containing the deepest, highest levels of the *ein sof*, fell and eventually trickled down into our physical reality. Our personal and collective task becomes to locate the sparks and elevate them, which we will explore shortly in Gate 10, the discussion of *birur*, sifting and *tikun*, repairing.

✤ In our youth, our energy can be too intense and cause a breakdown—within ourselves, or between ourselves and others—mirroring the shattering of the vessels. We achieve genuine healing when we reclaim the intensity of our youth and contain it within a mature, tempered vessel.

GATE 8

Tohu & Tikun
Chaos & Order

After the initial *tzimtzum*, compartmentalized reality emerged slowly. Following the *tzimtzum*, a world of *akudim*, ringed reality, came into focus. In this field of reality, the *sefiros* are a unified whole, all the light bound in one vessel. There was no distinction between the *sefiros* on this level. The world was one of *yuli*, potential reality.

Next emerged the world of *nekudim*, spotted or dotted reality, a world with evident distinctions and clear individuality. Here, each *sefira* feels its own importance, and remains aloof from the others. As the Infinite undergoes *tzimtzum* to allow the finite, each *sefira* seizes the opportunity to express itself fully without regard to the other *sefiros* and cacophony ensues. The state of this world is strong *yeshus*—I/existence/ego—and thus it is perpetually in a condition of *tohu*, chaos and confusion.

We find this in the behavior of children when they feel overlooked during adult conversation: The moment they receive the attention they crave, they grab center stage and steal the show. The child is protecting his still fragile ego, as is developmentally appropriate.

Next, after potential and chaos, came the world of perfect order, *tikun*. This world is also referred to as *verudim*, flecked existence. Here, each of the *sefiros* are properly balanced between fully expressing their individuality and also connecting with the others. The vessels have matured and are more 'humble.' There even the possibility of *achlifu duchtaihu*, exchanging places,

---

where the light of one *sefira* transfers into another.

❧ We can see these three stages reflected in human development. .

◖ *Akudim:* From birth, everything an infant sees is viewed as an extension of himself, there are no separations or distinctions. This is a pre-personal stage.

◖ *Nekudim:* The next stage is where the child becomes aware of his separate body, and the ego takes charge. He is in *yeshus* mode, and believes that the whole world revolves around him. This is a personal stage

◖ *Verudim:* With maturity one attains a fresh attitude: We coexist as individuals within a greater unity. This is the world of *tikun*, a trans-personal stage.

GATE 9

Kelipa - Concealment

The *'first tzimtzum'*—the original primordial retraction of the infinite light—brought the concept of *kelipa* into being.

The word *kelipa* is translated as a "shell, husk or covering." *Kelipa* refers to all forces of negativity.

Negativity conceals the *ohr ein sof* as if encasing it in a husk.

On a personal level, when we undergo a positive experience, we can connect it to "the light"—its divine source, purpose and meaning. However, when confronted with tragedy, we see it as negative. When we are in pain, we are disconnected from the light; we do not observe the reason or the wisdom in the event. Our experience is the 'vessel' (outer shell), and the positive purposeful lesson or direction is the 'light' within.

In terms of our relationship with observable reality we are capable of both *kelipa* and non-*kelipa* perception. At times, we perceive the light clearly, as the hand of the Creator guiding our life. At other times, all we observe is the outer representation, the husk, and feel separated from the light. Occasionally we linger and vacillate between both perceptions; between observing the light and being obstructed by the vessels, the husk of our experience.

One kind of *kelipa* is referred to as *shalash kelipos,* three *kelipas*/husks. There is another *kelipa* of *nogah*, glowing husk. In the former, the vessels (also a symbol for experience) are so dense that we do not sense the light at all. In the latter, what we notice first is the façade, yet we perceive a glow within that suggests a deeper reality.

The "three" of *shalash kelipos* refers to the three central elements of creation: fire, wind and water—the fourth element, earth, is included in the previous three.

❧ When we take a non-mindful look at material existence, it appears separate from its Source; the vessel is disengaged from the light. This occurs because of *tzimtzum*: The light has been sidelined as the vessels have taken prominence in our perspective. At this denser level of *kelipa*, it is very challenging to perceive the light. In the *nogah* paradigm, the light is still dimly perceived.

A reorientation is required on the part of the observer so that he or she can recognize the light and not get trapped in the world of matter which obscures the world of spirit.

GATE 10

Birur & Hala'as Ha'netzutzim
Sifting & Elevating the Sparks

There are *ra'pach netzutzim*—two hundred and eighty eight general clusters of sparks from the "broken vessels" scattered throughout our created observable reality. In this world of substance, where everything lies within particular dimensions of time and space, sparks of the infinite endless light are covered over and concealed from immediate perception.

Within the physical and spiritual brokenness around us, there are intense holy sparks waiting to be sifted out and released.

It becomes our task in this world to repair, sift out and elevate the sparks to their Source in holiness. By recreating that which has been destroyed, and repairing that which has become broken, we bring *tikun*—order, healing and meaning—to a world of chaos and confusion, an even greater *tikun* than before the original breaking.

There is personal *tikun*, rectification, and *tikun olam*, global rectification. Our mission is to repair our personal broken vessels; to work on ourselves to mend our character flaws. The very reason our perfect souls "embody" is so that we can perform the transformative act of refining our natural temperaments as a personal *tikun*.

As a result of our individual elevation and repair, we can in-

---

spire a *tikun* upon our immediate surroundings. Ripples of our actions cause a *tikun olam*, a restoration of the entire world.

The Torah distinguishes between permitted and forbidden actions. A permitted action, for example, is "earning a living." A forbidden one is "stealing." The permitted actions themselves may be elevated through *hislabshus*—involvement. When we earn our wages with integrity and honesty, we elevate the sparks contained within our earnings. By engaging with proper mindfulness and divine intention, the sparks become more accessible to retrieval.

Everything contains sparks. Objects or actions that are hurtful, mean-spirited, or excessive only appear this way because their sparks are deeply obscured within the mask of *kelipa*. In such cases, the sparks are released through disengagement—referred to as *dechiya*—pushing aside. Refraining from negative actions or mindsets liberates the sparks and allows for *tikun*. For example, refraining from expressing anger releases the spark within the anger. Eating a healthy meal raises the sparks within food, but refraining from overeating releases sparks too.

❧ We each have sparks to which we gravitate. Some of us are attracted to certain foods, music and people, while others gravitate towards other foods, music or people. Each person is pulled towards the sparks that are connected to their soul's purpose and destiny. Personal *tikun* comes from listening to our deeper calling, It occurs when we follow the positive aspects of our personality with all the strength of our being and refrain from negative behaviors with equal perseverance.

GATE II

Ohr Sovev & Ohr Memale
The Light that Surrounds and Light that Fills Creation

There is the *ohr ha'sovev kol almim*—the light that surrounds all worlds, and the *ohr memale kol almim*—the light that fills all creation. The Creator's energy manifested as both an immanent and transcendent force. *Memale* is a light which "fills" the universe, permeating all creation. *Sovev* is the light that "encompasses" and hovers above creation.

Clearly these images of surrounding and filling are not to be taken literally. They are strictly related to the degree of their revelation and manifestation in the universe. The divine light that is revealed within the physical is referred to as *memale*—filling the world. This light can be experienced as the Creator orchestrating the details of our lives. The divine light that is less revealed is called *sovev*—encompassing. This light is revealed at times of awe when we sense that there is much beyond what we can easily understand or articulate.

In the process of creation, the infinite *sovev* generates the substance, the actual "thing," while *memale* configures it into a particular form. Existence comes from *sovev* and structure and animation from *memale*. The light of *memale* is intimately vested in the universe much as a soul is clothed with a body. The light of *sovev* creates the body itself.

In our own creative process, the object begins with our

inspiration, but is actually materialized by our perspiration. When we are moved to create, there is an *infinite* desire that gushes forth, compelling us, this is similar to *sovev*, yet, in order to actually create we need a detailed *finite* structure like *memale* provides, be it an instrument or canvas. We need both the infinite creativity of *sovev* and the finite implementation of *memale*.

In the world of *memale* the natural flow is rigid and predictable. We are born with a certain set of genes, into a particular setting and environment. A person's life might simply be lived in reaction to these fixed details. When we submit to conditioning, and allow our behavior to be determined by factors, we find ourselves within the realm of *memale*. This is life lived in a passive manner.

Thankfully, there is more to the story.

❧ Deep within us we harbor the light of *sovev*—the infinite creative aspect, which gives us the ability to transcend our environment and genetic makeup. We have within us the power to push past our personal limitations and choose to harness infinity and become the creators of our own lives.

GATE 12

Kudsha Berich Hu & the Shechina
The Male and Female Dynamic

There is a traditional Kabbalistic prayer that is chanted at the start of a new day or before the performance of a *mitzvah*, a sacred act. It is called the *le'sheim yichud*—for the purpose of unification. In it we say: "For the sake of unity between *Kudsha Berich Hu*—the Holy One Blessed by He—and *Shechintei*—His *Shechinah*: the indwelling Presence."

Berich Hu, "Blessed be He," represents the masculine, detached, transcendent aspect of divine energy that remains unmoved by human action or inaction. The feminine *Shechinah* represents that which is *shochen*—dwelling among, permeating, finite and immediate.

As physical creations of this world, our actions influence the intensity of the *Shechinah*. Our positive acts "elevate the *Shechinah*" and our negative acts cause the *Shechinah* to "fall." We are the "limbs of the *Shechinah*."

Our negative actions not only alienate our conscious self from the divine light within us, but they have cosmic repercussions as well: We diminish the Divine *memale* light apportioned to existence, distorting, as well as reducing, the Divine energy immanent within creation. Thus, any time we are in personal exile, the *Shechina* is in exile as well. Conversely, when we are redeemed there is also redemption for the *Shechinah*.

The cosmic fall of the *Shechinah* deepens the disunity between the *Shechinah* (female) and *Berich Hu* (male) aspects of the Creator. In order to replenish and uplift the finite *Shechina,* we need to access the limitless *Berich Hu,* the infinite divine energy that encompasses creation. When we perform a *mitzvah,* a transcendent "infinite" noble act, we reach for the infinite and inspire unity, *yichud,* between *Kudsha Berich Hu* and *Shechinah.*

The recitation of the *yichud* prayer affirms awareness of our actions, and facilitates the connection between the immanent and transcendent aspect of the Creator.

❧ On a personal level, we perform a *yichud* when our internal feelings are perfectly reflected by our external actions.

GATE 13

Osyos
Sounds, Vibrations &
Letters

We use language to transmit thoughts and information. On a deeper level, our words create reality. In this way, our language dimly reflects Divine language which transmits the divine energy of Creation. The book of Genesis describes this process: "G-d said let there be... and there was...." Divine words created the world.

Everything in our universe has a unique space, structure, sound and rhythm. Everything has a distinctive kind of vibration. The "things" we observe with our senses are physical manifestations of their respective divine frequencies. In fact, in Hebrew there is no word for "thing." Is is merely called *de'var*—word, or utterance. Every "thing" is truly the product of a unique divine vibration.

Letters are called *osyos* related to the words *asa boker*—the day has come. The letters reveal light. And letters are also called "horses" as they carry and transmit divine energy into each particular vessel, each physical representation.

Essentially, "things" are "words." It follows then, that when two words share similar sounds or letters, a deeper spiritual association exists between the two items. Even if two words are related merely because they contain the same letters, albeit in a different sequence, this too suggests kinship. What is more, adding up the numeric values of the letters, the *gema-*

---

triya, numerical equivalent, can also give clues to relationship. Every letter possesses a specific numeric value. Calculating the number value of two words can deepen understanding of their connection to one another.

The word *gematriya* can be divided in two, *gai*—number in Greek—and *matria*—wisdom. In Hebrew, *gai* means "valley" and in Aramaic, *matria* means "mountain." The mountain is created from the earth of the valley, thus the mountain and the valley are mirror images.

The system of *gematriya* is complex. Sometimes letters that have similar sounds—or sounds that emanate from the same location in the mouth (such as guttural sounds)—are exchanged. There are times when the first letter of the *aleph beis* (Hebrew alphabet) is exchanged with the last letter of the *aleph beis*, and the second with the second to the last, and so on. There are times when only the 'revealed' letters are taken into account, and there are times when the letters are expanded and the entire *milui*—filling of the word is taken into account.

The significance of *gematriya* lies not in the numerical match-up. Rather, the numerical equivalence points to a cosmological truth. It is an outward expression of a deeper connection between the two words.

When a parallel is drawn in the Talmud or Zohar it is because the sages grasped a profound connection between two ideas—only afterwards were equivalencies sought in their external representation. Therefore, just because A equals or sounds like B does not mean that they are deeply connected.

For example, the *gematriya* of the name Moshe (Moses) is 345. This number is equivalent to two sacred names of G-d in the Torah: *Shad-ai* (314) and *E-l* (31). However, it *also* has the numerical equivalent of "other deities," *elokim* (86) *acherim* (259).

☙ If one is not well versed in this discipline, it is best not to attempt it. Certainly, one's life decisions should not be based on the result of this kind of numerology.

GATE 14

Sefiros
From One to Many

There were ten hidden *sefiros* before the *tzimtzum*. The vessels (the *sefiros*) existed even before the primordial contraction. It was only when the *ohr ein sof*, Infinite light, contracted that the finite was able to appear and not be overwhelmed. When the *tzimtzum* occurred (and continued to re-occur), a linear, up-and-down sequential structure emerged.

The ten *sefiros* are like ten screens through which the Infinite light of the *ein sof* penetrates our finite reality. The distinct forms, shapes and colors of the *sefiros* serve as filters through which the infinite colorless, formless, unified light is reflected into our world. Passing through the *sefiros* causes the light to appear differentiated and colored.

The order of the *sefiros* is as follows:

The first to arise is the *sefira* of *keser*, the crown, which is expressed as deep desire and the primordial will of the infinite to create that which is finite.

Then comes the *sefiros* of intellect, *chochmah*, wisdom and intuition, and *binah*, reason and cognition. When *keser* is not counted among the ten, *da'as*, knowledge and awareness, is. Collectively, these three aspects of the intellect are referred to as *cha'bad*.

Next come the three primary internal emotions—*cha'gas*. On the right, expansive column is *chesed*—kindness and love. On the left, restrictive column is *gevurah*—strength and restraint. Between *chesed* and *gevurah* is their synthesis, *tiferes*—compassion and beauty. *Tiferes* is giving with sensitivity to the needs of the recipient. This is true compassion, which creates harmony and beauty, and is the synthesis between giving all and withholding completely.

The 'outer' implementing emotions, the *Ne'hi*, are also divided into three. On the right, expansive column is *netzach*—victory and ambition. On the left column is *hod*—humility and devotion, and in the middle is the unifying agent, connecting the giver and the receiver: the idea of *yesod*—foundation and relationship.

Malchus, kingship, is receptiveness. It represents the vessel that receives from the preceding nine *sefiros.* It re-channels the energies downward, thus becoming the 'crown' for the subsequent structure of *sefiros,* as the image of ten keeps on replicating throughout all realities.

These cosmic vessels are the basic tools of creation, and the basic tools of our own creative efforts. We are a part of this great chain of the creative process and the *sefiros* are embodied within us as well. On the cosmic level, formless oneness emerges into full formed structure through ten sefirotic stages.

❧ On the human level, we pass through similar processes. Our emergence from unified consciousness into a world of duality and polarity begins with an internal desire or will for relationship, which eventually becomes rationalized and understood on an intellectual level. Ultimately, it is articulated as full emotion as we enter into a "real" relationship with the other. As we flow from oneness to multiplicity, let us remember our purpose to bring our newfound wisdom back into the one, and on a deeper level, to reveal the Unity within diversity.

Keser—desire; super-conscious

Chochmah—wisdom; intuition
Binah—reason; cognition
Da'as—knowledge; awareness
Chesed—kindness; love
Gevurah—strength; restraint
Tiferes—compassion; beauty
Netzach—victory; ambition
Hod—devotion; humility
Yesod—foundation; relationship
Malchus—royalty; receptiveness

GATE 15

Da'as Elyon & Tachton
Higher and Lower
Awareness

The Zohar teaches that when *keser* is counted among the ten *sefiros* then *da'as* is not and when *da'as* is counted *keser* is not.

The higher *sefira, keser,* fosters the development of a meta-level of cognition that allows the person to house the fundamental paradoxes of life; encompassing and connecting the various dimensions of reality.

Da'as is knowledge. Knowledge is the internalization of a thought; it is the place which is responsible for judgment and planning. Choices and implementations occur in *da'as*. Until opinions, notions, ideas and concepts become absorbed in *da'as,* they remain abstract and inconsequential.

Da'as is also the bridge between our thoughts and feelings.

Da'as and *keser* are interchangeable, as they represent alternative expressions of the same unifying force. *Da'as* unifies our thoughts and connects them to our feelings, creating the ability to choose accordingly.

Da'as is comprised of two levels; *elyon*-higher and *tachton*-lower.

Cosmically, *da'as elyon,* higher *da'as,* otherwise known as *da'as ha'nelam,* reserved *da'as,* represents non-duality, a position in which the flow of time and the multi dimensionality of space do not exist. *Da'as tachton,* lower *da'as* otherwise known as *da'as ha'mispashet, da'as* that extends outward represents a condition in

---

which "otherness" does exist, yet it feels itself humbled by its Source. When we function on a *da'as elyon* reality we no longer feel ourselves separate from our Source, in fact, we no longer feel. We are one with the Unity. However, when we function in a *tachton* condition, we feel our existence, and within that reality we seek a relationship with our Creator.

The difference between *elyon* and *tachton* is the difference between context and content. In *elyon*, there is nothing prior; our choice creates the template. In *tachton*, the context already exists and our choices fill in the details.

Elyon is creative and comprehensive. It is in this domain that we choose our purpose and life trajectory. *Tachton* choices are the ones we make in order to meet the goals established in the state of *elyon*.

For example, an *elyon* statement would be, "I want to be a doctor." A corresponding *tachton* statement would be: "I want to go to this particular medical school."

❧ Often people go through life on the level of *tachton*. The context of their lives has been already chosen for them, either by parents, schooling, upbringing, or environment. Their time is spent filling a previously selected canvas.

Dipping into the non-dualistic, cosmic *elyon* allows one to break free of pre-existing context and recreate life anew, with openness, empowerment and boundless joy.

GATE 16

Partzuf - Divine Personae

The *sefiros* are like holographic images, each one reflects itself and contains traces of the other nine. They are further grouped into *partzufim*—personae or profiles. Each *partzuf* contains the pattern of the entire ten. The *sefiros* are not only individual manifestations of divine attributes, but also are positioned in various configurations, visages or profiles.

There are a total of five *partzufim*.

❧ *Atik-keser* is detached, transcendent reality.

❧ *Arich anpin* is "long, enlarged face" which later becomes *keser*, the crown that influences that which it rests upon.

❧ *A'v'a* is a contraction of the two words, *aba,* father, and *ima,* mother. Father and mother represent the two cognitive *sefiros: chochmah,* wisdom, is the masculine father who provides the kernel which impregnates *binah,* reason, the feminine mother who nurtures the thought into a full-grown expanded idea.

❧ *Zeir anpin*—"small, constricted face," the emotional *sefiros.*

❧ *Nukvah*—the feminine, the receiver which is also the vessel that contains the flow and transmits it into the next group of five.

Each *partzuf* contains the entire arrangement of all the *sefiros,* albeit, occasionally in a *zeir,* a smaller, contracted version, so that each one is a total structure, a full divine persona. For example, in the universe of emotions there is also intelligence: the intellect guides and orients the emotions. Similarly, in the world of intelligence there are also emotions, which stir and affect all understanding.

❧ In our own lives, we need to experience the blending of *sefiros*. If we don't, we might feel, for example, the tremendous pain of another in need, but we will lack the *mindfulness* to gather the resources to create the desired result.

Even within the *partzufim* we always need to strike the perfect blend. Take, for example the *sefira* of *chesed*—giving, and now imagine it without a trace of *gevurah*—restraint. In a state of pure *chesed,* if you saw a child playing with a knife you might simply smile and allow him to continue. But the situation demands that you is to show some *gevurah* and take the knife from the child.

Overall, we aim for balance. Integrating the *sefiros* requires adjusting ourselves to equilibrium. The ideal is to conduct ourselves with intuition tempered by reason, with kindness and sensitivity to the other, and with our self-esteem and ambition bounded by proper humility and dedication.

GATE 17

Adam Kadmon
Primordial Likeness

There are the four progressive spiritual worlds, each reflected in aspects of the "body" and then there is the body itself, *Adam kadmon*—"primordial man"—the space in which all details exist as one. *Adam kadmon* is the context of our (and all) being, a context that contains and embraces both the infinite *ayin*—emptiness, no-thingness, and the finite *yesh*—existence, of the lower three worlds.

Adam, man, comes from the word *domeh,* "in the image," rooted also in the word *dimyon,* "imagination."

"*Kadmon*" means primary or primordial.

The world of *Adam kadmon* is the world of *kesarim* (plural form of *keser*)—the original desire and primordial will in which the Infinite Oneness desired a relationship with a created finite "other."

The perfect imagination of the Infinite dreamt up a finite creation whose potential would eventually be fully articulated in its final, finite form through the process of the four worlds. In the primordial condition of infinite desire all finite existence retains its perfect state—a true "likeness of" the infinite light.

♣ We are all rooted in the primordial likeness of the Creator. Our actions do not always reflect this basic truth. We are always presented with the choice to remain fixed upon the externals, or to try to peek a bit deeper and see others as they exist in *Adam kadmon,* in their perfectly transcendent and noble potential.

GATE 18

Atzilus - Unified Reality

There are four worlds, one above the other and one within the other: *azílus*—closeness, *beriah*—creation, *yetzirah*—formation, and *asiyah*—actualization.

The four worlds represent four perspectives. The highest perspective is that of "light" and the lowest is that of "vessel." Light suggests meaning, purpose and value. Vessel suggests density, lack of meaning and purposeless.

We can see our lives as full of light, meaning, and purpose, or we can constrict our perception to the level of "vessel," connoting nothing deeper than what is immediately observable. A sack of potatoes may have the same net weight as your child. Yet when you carry your child, you are less attuned to the "vessel," the physical weight, as you are to the "light," the feeling for the one in your arms.

From *keser*—desire, potential, from *Adam kadmon*—primordial likeness, comes the first of the four worlds, the world of *atzilus*. From the Hebrew word *etzel*—near, *atzilus* is a world that is close enough to its source to have no perceived existence of its own.

Atzilus is the world of intuition, corresponding to silence.

The emanation of *atzilus* is totally dissolved in its source of emanation. This radical being/nothingness is referred to as *bitul be'metziyus*—nullification of existence. Here "The light and the vessel are one." The Infinite Source (*ohr ein sof*) and its receptacle are fused together.

In terms of the *sefiros*, *keser*—desire, is reflected in *Adom kad-*

mon, and *chochmah*—wisdom and intuition, is represented in *atzilus*. First there is the divine desire to create otherness, and when this desire begins to assume form, there is already an intuition of how this desire will be articulated and brought to fruition.

There are four letters in the Name of G-d, the Tetragrammaton, otherwise known as "*Havaya*." The first of the four letters, the *yud* (י), predominates in the realm *atzilus*. *Yud* is the initial kernel of thought, the intuition before it is formulated into detailed description.

❧ Attaining *bitul be'metziyus*, the total negation of separate existence, does not render the person worthless and inconsequential. On the contrary, one becomes "more" by being "less." Once an individual is no longer bounded by ego, a finite separate self, he or she can become even "more," an infinite expansive instrument for the Everything.

GATE 19

Beriah - Separate Reality

The worlds *atzilus* and above are from a reality known as *alma d'iskasya*—the hidden world. The divine light of the upper worlds are transcendent, infinite, and beyond the grasp of the finite mechanism of the dualistic brain. Beginning with the world of *beriah*, continuing through the worlds of *yetzirah* and *asiya*, is the *alma d'isgalya*, the revealed world, with its hallmarks of finitude and potential for human comprehension and interaction.

Until this point of the ever unfolding creative process, the idea of having something apparently "outside the infinite Oneness" was a mere glimmer of desire *within* the mind of the *ein sof*—hence, there is no real separation. It with *beriah* that radical separation occurs, and "otherness" begins to assume some of the properties of *yesh*, of physicality.

The world of *beriah* is the world in which occurs the actual creation of *yesh*, something, from divine *ayin*, nothing. This is called creation of *yesh m'ayin*: some-thing from no-thing.

The Torah opens with the words "*Bereishis bara Elokim*—In the beginning G-d created." The word the Torah uses for "creation" is *bara*, a word that implies a "new" creation *ex nihilo*, from nothing.

Bara also means "cut off." In the world of *beriah* there is a radical cutting off from the divine Source. *Bara* also comes from the word *bar*, outside, because created physical reality appears to exist outside of spiritual divine Unity.

The notion of creating a *yesh* is encoded within the first

word of the Torah, *"Bereishis."* Rearranging the letters of this word, the word can spell *bara'sa yesh,* creating something, the beginning of the reality of separateness.

In the process of creation, first there is the desire, then the glimmer in the mind, then the actuality of its creation as the "vessel" begins to separate from the Light.

Beriah is the world of thought, corresponding to breath.

The *sefira* of *binah,* reason, is most pronounced in the world of *beriah. Binah* is where the unpacking of *chochmah,* wisdom, occurs. *Binah* provides the ability to absorb the ambiguous seed of *chochmah* and articulate it into comprehensive detail. For this reason the Torah employs speech as the metaphor when describing of the process of *bara*—creating the physical world. "G-d said let there be light... and there was light." As a thought that is spoken assumes form, creation is manifested in speech.

As the *yud* (ʼ) is connected to *atzilus,* the second letter of G-d's name, the letter *hei* (ה), is associated with *beriah.* Unlike the small, contained letter *yud,* the letter *hei* has more body, it extends vertically and horizontally. *Beriah* is where the progression of time and space begins to form.

This movement from *atzilus* into *beriah* should not be over-simplified into a progression on a time line. Rather, creation is a continuing process in which there are levels of *atzilus, beriah, yetzirah* and *asiya.*

❧ The delicate moment of self-consciousness in *beriah* is marked by *bitul ha'yesh,* nullification of what *is* (separate physical existence). Functioning on a *beriah* level, we become aware of ourselves as fully *"yesh."* And since *beriah* is the first movement away from unified reality, *beriah* consciousness is characterized by deep relation to, and detachment from, our Source. In *beriah,* we are humbled and nullified by the awareness of our separateness.

GATE 20

Yetzirah - Formed Reality

As physicality slowly materializes, first it shows up as *chomer*, substance, within the world of *beriah*. Within the world of *Yetzirah*, the realm of formation, substance later assumes *tzurah*, individuated form.

In the world of *beriah* there is substance but no individuation. All of creation, including time, the galaxies and their vast space, all life, all of us and everything are lumped together as one lump of undifferentiated material. Within the realm of *Yetzirah*, distinct forms begin to emerge from this material.

Yetzirah is from the word *yatzar*, to form. What occurs in *yetzirah* is not a "new" creation, but rather a forming of what already exists. In the Torah's first chapter, the verb that is used to describe the main action is *bara*, "created." In the Torah's second chapter, the term switches to *yatzar*, "formed." Once creation of a physical world has taken place, it becomes time for matter to assume its proper formation. *Yesh* is altered into its own particular *yeshus*, selfhood.

Think of it in terms of your own creations. First you have an idea. Then you assemble all the necessary materials to implement your idea. Only when everything is together do you begin to separate materials and use each one for its own particular purpose.

Yetzirah is the world of speech, corresponding to sound.

The emotional attributes of *cha'gas* (*chesed, gevurah* and *tiferes*) and *ne'hi* (*netzach, hod* and *yesod*), the six primary emotional *sefiros*, are most apparent in the world of *yetzirah*. The six emotions can only exist within a paradigm of relationship. Whether these six emotions are used to extend oneself or to hold oneself aloof, they demand separation; the idea that there is another to whom we are relating. Because *yetzirah* is more "separate" from its Source than *beriah*, the emotional *sefiros* are more pronounced.

As the six emotional *sefiros* are most present in *yetzirah,* the letter that is embodied within this sphere of reality is the *vav* (ו). *Vav* is the sixth letter of the Hebrew alphabet, reflecting the six emotions. Because the letter itself is a vertical column, it also represents a movement downward and outward; downward into the body and outward towards another person.

Angels "reside", for the most part in *yetzirah*. The collective image of angels is that of singing, excitement and movement. *Yetzirah* is a universe of emotion. Here, separation from the Source is keenly felt, and there is a correspondingly profound and pure yearning to reunite with the One.

⁂ When we experience a pure transcendent emotion that lifts us out of our ordinary, time-bound reality, we move into an angelic realm. When we rise up in song, when music transports us, our consciousness is in a state of *yetzirah*.

GATE 21

Asiya - Physical Reality

Once substance and form fuse together, the end result is the physical material world we apprehend with our five senses. *Asiya* is the world of action and completion. It is only within *asiya* that definitions of absolute time and space take hold.

Asiya is the embodiment of *malchus*. This is the divine feminine aspect within the *sefiros*, the *Shechina*. It is also the receptacle of blessing from the higher *sefiros*, which disseminates the blessing to the worlds below.

The earth is the end receiver of the divine plenty and blessing. "In the beginning G-d created heavens (the spirit), and earth (the physical)." The final *hei* (ה) of G-d's name is related to *Asiya* and is expressed in the multi-dimensionality of this universe. As the letter *hei* expands vertically and horizontally, the physical world expands into time, from the present into the future, and flows into the six directions of space.

Asiya implies action, the product of the preliminary desire and dream. When the divine desire was awakened for the creation of "otherness," it projected a vision of the end product. When an architect plans to build a structure, he first imagines how it will look once it is built. He starts with a mental image, and then goes through the process of creating the building in physical space. Only when the structure is completed has the original dream been actualized.

Asiyah is the world of action, corresponding to voice.

Sof ma'ase machshava techila—the end of action is the original thought. The Essence of all reality, *atzmus* (otherwise known as the *yesh amiti*—true existence) is perceived to be more present in *yesh ha'nivra*, created existence, than within all other creations.

The physical world is spiritually unique in that it supports the illusion that it is self-referential and independent of a creator. All other realms are spiritually oriented, and there is a continuous exchange of energy from one world to the next. The physical universe, on the other hand, is not apparently linked to *yetzira, beriah* and certainly not *atzilus*. Only Essence—which was certainly not caused by any antecedent—has the capacity to produce a world that appears to be autonomous.

Only *atzmus*—whose being is an imperative and whose existence is derived from the Self—has the ability to yield a creation that is unaware that its existence is due to a creator. The creation feels that it has emerged into being on its own. Physicality is rooted in the deepest recesses within Essence. The end is truly embedded in the beginning.

❧ This is the power of actions. A simple act of goodness can be purer and more profound than all the loftiest thoughts and transcendent feelings. Even the smallest good action is connected with the Ultimate Simplicity, the Essence of all Reality.

GATE 22

Malachim - Angels

Within the teachings of the *kabbalah* there are the *ma'ase bereishis*, the inner-workings of creation, and the *ma'ase merkava*, the workings of "the chariot." The latter is a genre of spiritual teachings that primarily explore the function of angels.

But what are angels?

In simplest terms an angel is a messenger—a conduit of energy. Since everything carries a distinct energy, everything in life can be deemed angelic.

In fact, with every thought we entertain, every word we utter, and every action we perform, we release angels of energy. These energies are projected into the atmosphere around us. Positive thoughts, words and actions create positive vibes, whereas negativity projects negativity. Our energy field reflects who we are and how we behave.

Besides these personal (subjective) angels, there are cosmic (objective) angels that were created at the same time as the physical world. The purpose of these angels is to receive the Divine life force from one realm and transmit it to another. In this way, angels act as channels through which the energy of the universe flows downwards and upwards.

Cosmic angels are pure spirit and can only be sensed in a meditative trance state, with the help of insight from the "third eye." These angels are thus identified with the intangible physical property, light. Occasionally, these energy forces may "lower themselves" and vest within physical form.

There are four primary elements to physical matter: fire, wind, water and soil. They can also be classified as: heat, moisture, cold and dryness. In modern scientific language these may be hydrogen, nitrogen, oxygen and carbon. The fire, wind, water and earth are not meant to be taken literally as clods of earth, buckets of water, air in the atmosphere, or a flame on a candle. Rather, these are to be regarded as a primary forms of matter.

An angel may become embodied in primary matter. Angels may take a form in fire, for instance, or a blend of elements, such as fire together with wind. In this form, the angel would be sensed as a type of apparition or silhouette. An angel may even assume a *malbush*, a garment, comprised of all four elements and become readily apparent even to the untrained eye.

There are three groups of angels: *seraphim*—fiery ones, *chayos*—lively ones, and *ofanim*—wheels. The three groups correspond respectively to the three worlds of *beriah*, *yetzirah* and *asiya*.

Seraphim are connected with the world of *beriah*. *Seraphim* are angels that are totally consumed by an awareness of the Infinite and thus by the paradox of finitude emerging from Infinity. *Chayos* are connected with the emotional universe of *yetzirah*, an energy field of emotional response to the downward flow of Divine Energy. *Ophanim* are connected with *asiya*, the world of action. *Ophanim* are the wheels. Wheels reduce the friction between the riding vehicle and the earth; so, too, *ophanim* serve as a smooth interface between the non-physical *beriah* and *yetzirah* and the total physicality of *asiya*.

During his mystical vision, Ezekiel perceived an *ophan* upon the earth. The Talmud explains this as a description of an angel named *Sandalphon* who stands on the earth and whose head reaches the *chayos*. The root of the word *sandalphon* is *sandal*, shoe. This angel acts as the shoes of the divine presence resting in this world. *Sandalphon* allows the integration between spiritual life energy and material physical matter.

Sandalphon also refers to "lower intelligence." *Sandal* refers to the *golem*—unshaped form, of objects, and *"phon"* means "turned toward." The act of creativity in the realm of physical substance occurs when we turn our intellect toward an object. Our ability to create art resembles that of *ophanim/sandalphon*.

♣ When we experience a pure, transcendent clarity of thought beyond our own egos, a fiery overwhelming awareness of the unity of the Creator, we are experiencing *seraphim*. When we experience emotions that are elevated, noble, completely dedicated, focused and oriented towards our Source, we are experiencing *chayos*. Finally, when our hearts and minds are more engaged in the physical, we are like *ophanim*.

Every phenomenon we encounter has its physical explanation, as well as its "angel," a spiritual interpretation or lesson. And every single life experience carries energy, and is therefore an angel. When experiences open us up to love, mindfulness, and more alignment with our Source, the angelic message is a positive one. Conversely, when experiences are stifling, leave us feeling closed, in disarray, disconnected and alienated, then the angel carries a message of concealment and negativity. This leads us to the next gate, the exploration of negative forces.

GATE 23

Ruchos
Negative Forces, Demons &
the Angel of Death

Angels are transmitters of energy, facilitating the smooth transition from the spiritual to the physical and visa versa—from the Unity into the multiplicity and from multiplicity back into the Unity. Negativity is engendered when that energy flow is blocked. *Ruchos*, spirits, *sheidim*, demons, *malach ha'maves*, the angel of death, and *Satan* are defective transmitters which cause a negative distortion of the divine flow of energy.

Ever since the *tzimtzum*, the cosmic contraction of the infinite unified light, and man's involvement with the "tree of knowledge of good and evil" (the tree of opposites, polarity and duality), many of us labor under the illusion of separation. We perceive a splintered reality, whether in time, space or soul.

We assume time is broken down into many smaller units, and so is space and soul. In our constricted consciousness we believe that there is a definite past, a clear present and an eventual future, and that these three are vaguely connected. We also look around and see directions, and dimensions all with binary oppositions, a here and there, up and down, right or left. In the midst of all this multiplicity, there is a nebulous notion of the interconnectedness of all.

The *yetzer hara,* the ego or evil orientation, is *Satan* and the angel of death. These are all one and the same. The ego creates a boundary between self and the other, the concept of "angel of death" reflects an energy that dramatically separates life from afterlife, and *Satan* is the collective objective creation of all negativity, and these are one and the same. When we come to life from an ego/selfish you *or* me perspective, as opposed to a soul/transcendent/selfless perspective, we are choosing separateness. This reflects "tree of knowledge, of good or evil" discrimination, rather than unity, plucked from the "tree of life."

Kedushah, purity, holiness, is life, fluidity, movement and growth. Alternatively, *tuma*, impurity, is created within a context of death and rigidity. A lifeless body spreads *tuma*. The word *tuma* comes from the word *satum*, closed off, concealed, as it reflects a condition of separation and stagnation.

Tuma is *kelipa*, a shell. It blocks the divine animating, enlivening, creative force. In the apprehended world of separateness, the "tree of knowledge" model, where death is seen as the "end" of life, a body that dies is considered to bring *tuma*. When one who cleaves to the "tree of life" passes on, they do so with a divine kiss. The angel of death has no mastery over them, and their bodies are pure and holy as the time before their souls left their bodies.

When our perception of time is divided into a past, present and future, our perceptions emanate from a space of fragmented consciousness. *Satan*-like consciousness goes one step further and past time is perceived as unrelated to present, or future. In this paradigm, we don't live in the eternal moment.

The Talmud relates that the Hebrew word *ha'Satan*, the Satan, has the number equivalent of three hundred and sixty four. As there are three sixty five days in solar calendar, this suggests that there is one day that stands outside the grip of *Satan*, and that is *Yom Kippur.* Known as the day of atonement, *Yom Kippur* is referred to as *achas ba'shanah*—oneness of year. *Achas ba'shanah* can also be translated as the oneness within the *shinui*, the changing. Changing connotes diversity and division, and *Yom Kippur* gives us the ability to break free of our ego's separate consciousness and dip into transcendence, a unified reality of oneness.

The embodiment of all *tuma* is referred to as the angel *Sam-e-l*. *Sam* is the Hebrew word for poison, and *e-l* is Torah's name for G-d's aspect of *chesed*, the Source of goodness. *Sam-e-l* is the poisoning of the Divine energy flow, restricting, limiting and preventing the appearance of Unity.

Within *Sam-e-l*, the negativity of the Name of God, are the letters *samach* (ס), and final *mem* (ם). Among the letters of the Hebrew alphabet, the *samach* and final *mem* are the only letters to be geometrically completely closed. Here in this name, they represent a stoppage of the Divine energy flow. They prevent Divine goodness from being observed or appreciated.

The great Jewish philosopher Maimonides was absolutely correct when he dismissed all these ideas of negative forces as total falsehoods, figments of the imagination. They are false, fakes, nothing but masks concealing the truth of divine Unity. They are perceptions of *kelipa*, concealment and separation. The moment we choose to lift the mask and see the light within the darkness, the darkness disappears.

❧ In life we always have this choice: either to approach the experiences of life as (positive) angels, understanding that what appear to be obstacles are in reality opportunities for further growth; or we can reactively submit to life, and see every event as a *kelipa*, a concealment, and every obstacle as another setback. We can live from an expanded consciousness of unity, and experience everything in life with openness and love, or approach life from a constricted consciousness, and experience everything in life with trepidation and fear. Life can either open us up, expanding and enlarging us, or shut us down and make us smaller. The choice is ours.

GATE 24

Nefesh - Psyche

There are multiple levels of soul. Throughout life we fluctuate from a state of ego, where we sense ourselves individually finite, to a point where we reach infinity and absolute unity.

The level of soul known as *nefesh* is a reflection of the universe of *asiya*. The final letter *hei* (ה) in the Tetragrammaton, G-d's name, is connected to this, our personal level of soul. All sensory and bodily experiences are from *nefesh*.

Nefesh is connected with our blood, our liver, and digestive system. On an elementary level *nefesh* is our subtle bio energy. Because it is responsible for growth, *nefesh* is connected with the mouth, the instrument that articulates our thoughts and feelings.

Nefesh is the spirituality of the physical. It is functional consciousness and bodily awareness. The pleasure we derive from physical actions or sport is connected with *nefesh*.

♣ Our *nefesh* is innate bodily intelligence and is our raw natural instinct for healing, self-preservation and survival. The core ego is adaptive and essential. Sometimes mistaken as a negative force, a healthy ego ascertains our survival and ensures that we are not being used, abused or manipulated.

GATE 25

Ruach - Spirit

Nefesh is primarily interested in the preservation of the body and ego. *Ruach*, literally spirit, expands and enlarges us, and moves us further. *Ruach* is a more fluid energy than *nefesh*, and the more fluidity, the higher is the level of the soul.

Yetzirah, the world of formation, angels and emotions, is connected to the sixth Hebrew letter, *vav*, which stands for the six primary emotions that are reflected as our *ruach*. *Ruach* is more subtle than tangible perceived physicality. Emotions, devotional expressions, and creative self-expressions are part of *ruach*-consciousness. *Ruach*, which is also translated as wind, is connected with speech and expression.

Being moved by someone's kindness or a beautifully played piece of music propels us into *ruach*. On the map of the *sefiros*, *ruach* is associated with the attribute of *tiferes*—compassion and beauty. Compassion creates unity between two people. There is an exchange between a giver and receiver, and the giver is fully sensitive to the needs of the receiver. Beauty is created by a symphony of various sounds or colors. Beauty is created by color and contrast, thesis and antithesis which synthesize to form a more beautiful unified image or sound.

Ruach is also associated with the heart, the expansiveness of feeling and an ability to sense something greater beyond ourselves. Because the word *ruach*, wind, can also refer to breath, it is connected with the nose.

❧ *Ruach* opens us up beyond ourselves, allowing us to be

moved past our own egos and in turn, to move others. As *nefesh* is connected to physical sensation and pleasure, *ruach* allows us access to aesthetics, which can inspire us to lose our "little" selves, without fear, within something that seems much greater than us.

GATE 26

Neshamah - Soul

Beriah is where outward *yesh* creation begins. Once there is a created context, then the content, the formation—*yetzirah*—can take place. Similarly, emotions that arise within us are often preconditioned and founded on past experiences which created the context. Whether we feel moved or not depends on whether the content fits within the context.

Neshamah is our soul level that reflects the world of *beriah*. *Neshamah* allows us to experience freedom, uninfluenced and unencumbered by outside forces. *Neshamah* gives us the ability to choose our life, according to the deepest resources of our deepest selves.

More specifically, *neshamah* is linked with the *sefirah* of *binah*—the refined aspects of thought such as understanding, reason and meaning. Because *neshamah* is a mental activity, it is connected with the brain as *ruach* is connected to the heart. The upper *hei* of G-d's name represents the sphere of divine understanding, and *neshamah* is connected with that *hei*. *Neshamah* is the place of *kavanah*, intention.

Understanding is similar to the art of hearing. Piece by piece, information is digested until a complete idea is formed in the mind. Phonetically, the word *neshamah* is related to the word *nishmah*, to hear, and thus *neshamah* is linked with the physical instrument that allows us to hear, the ears.

Collectively, these three levels—*nefesh*, *ruach* and *neshamah*—constitute our normative consciousness.

❧ The higher and deeper we go in our consciousness, the more fully we live. In *neshamah* reality we are physically grounded, emotionally equipped, and intellectually prepared to live in full harmony with the deepest levels of ourselves—the divine transcendent aspect of our being.

GATE 27

Chaya - Life

Individual self is very much felt on a *nefesh, ruach* and even *neshamah* level. Pleasure, aesthetics and creativity are all distinct expressions or interpretations of our selfhood. These three jointly make up our *personal self*, as it were, our finite self. We refer to their collective acronym, *Naran*.

There is another part of self that is not so much directed towards our personal (finite) self, its preservation or articulation; rather, it is directed toward our (infinite) Source. *Chaya*—life force, is manifested as *ratzon*, will. When we will or want a particular thing, a *netiyas ha'nefesh*, an inclining of ourselves toward the wanted object, occurs. When we think, reason, feel or sense something, we are oriented around the self; but when we *will* something there is a shift of emphasis from subject to object, and the focus becomes our desire for this external object.

Chaya is conceptually "outside" of the body, a *makif*, a surrounding energy. *Chaya* is thus connected with the skull, the over arching crown that surrounds the brain. In *chaya,* the body "ends" and everything "above" immediate body begins. *Chaya* is a reflection of the first letter of G-d's name, the small letter *yud*. Like the shape of the letter *yud* (ʹ) which leaps upward, *chaya* is our *netiyas ha'nefesh*, our spiritual inclination, towards our Source.

Whereas *neshamah* is cognitive and logical, and its most pristine state shows us the door to Infinity, *chaya* is beyond "mind," opening the door to spiritual intuition where we sense our connection to our Source and discover the deep will to retain awareness of this connection.

Reflecting the cosmic order, *chaya* is *atzilus* within us. It is the *ayin*, the emptiness, nothingness, a lack of any somethingness.

Chaya is the unified reality where our vessels (minds) are in total unison and completely absorbed within the Light and a distinction between vessel and light can no longer be made.

❧ All levels of will are manifestations of *chaya*, but our truest, deepest and primary will is the will to maintain connectedness with our Source in the most observable of ways, even while being embodied in physical form and in a material vessel.

GATE 28

Yechidah - Uniqueness

Whereas *neshamah* intellectually shows us the door of transcendence and *chaya* opens the door and wills us upward and inward, *yechidah* reveals the self beyond the door as part of the transcendence. *Yechidah*, uniqueness or oneness, is in harmony with the Unity of all reality.

Yechidah is on one hand *makif ha'rachok*: distant encircling. One way of looking at *yechidah* is that it is a level in a system of a hierarchy; the infinite background of our finite existence, the infinite space upon which our *naran*, the finite expressions of soul, are projected.

On the other hand, *yechidah* is also the essence of our being, one with the Essence of all reality. *Yechidah* is our essence which is *beyond* and *includes* all paradigms of hierarchy, and non-hierarchy, being and non-being.

Yechidah is where a fusion between *nitzutz boreh*, a spark of the all inclusive Creator, and *nitzutz nivrah*, a spark of the finite creation, occurs. *Yechida* is the interface with the Infinite Source. It a level in terms of its finite *nivrah* element, and also not a level in terms of the infinite aspect of *boreh*.

In the cosmic "fifth" world, *Adam kadmon*, Primordial Man, is reflected as our *yechidah*, the totality of our being in its most pristine state. *Yechidah* is the *kotzo shel yud*—the small dot above the *yud* within G-d's Name. It is the highest point where the letter ends and reaches up into the empty space above the letter.

Yechidah-essence cannot be defined, quantified or contextualized. Nor can it be observed, understood, or experienced, because it is one with the ultimate Observer and Experiencer.

❧ Living from *yechidah* is our truest way of being. *Yechidah* is where our thoughts, words, and actions are in perfect harmony with the *keser*, the desire of the Creator. We are also in harmony with creation. From *yechidah* we come to see all human beings for what they really are, in their divine potential: infinite, pure and a particular expression of Infinity.

GATE 29

Gilgul
Reincarnation of Souls

Effectively, there are finite distinctive unique levels of self (*naran*), and there are parts of self that are infinite, "beyond body" and beyond distinctiveness. Our finite actions or inactions affect only the parts of self that are time-bound and finite. Thus, what is relevant to the conversation with regard to *gilgul nishamos*, reincarnated souls, is only the *nefesh, ruach*, and on some level *neshamah* (not *chaya*, and certainly not *yechidah*).

All varied expressions of personality are rooted within the "primordial soul of Adam." As the body mirrors the soul, there are souls today that are rooted in the head of "the soul of Adam," and there are souls who stem from the "hands of Adam," there are souls from the "heart," and souls from the "feet."

Ostensibly, "head souls" gravitate toward intellectual pursuit, whereas "hand souls" show signs of physical dexterity. "Heart souls" brim with emotions and "feet souls" are movement oriented. The genetic pattern of our physical bodies, together with the conditioning and contexts in which we grow (such as our environments and upbringing), are consistent with our particular soul- types. They fit and complement each other.

Because each image of the soul is complete, "head souls" are not without heart, and "heart souls" indeed have a portion of Primordial Adam's "head," or intelligence. Each distinct form possesses the complete capacity to think, feel work and move. Yet, one born with a "head soul" who instead occupies himself with "hand soul" concerns, is acting counter to his true nature, and thus will never be fully realized as a human being.

Ever since Man's fall from Eden and the identification with the "tree of good and evil," our task is to work on our collective and individual *tikun*, rectification. As a particular finite expression of self from within the "primordial soul of Adam" becomes embodied in physical form, its task is to fully actualize its distinct soul potential.

Through thoughts, words, acts of kindness, and the fulfillment of commandments, our particular authentic self can be repaired and shine brightly, first on the level of *nefesh*, then *ruach,* and later, *neshamah.* We each need to follow the path of our own brilliance in our own distinctive way.

Each of us possesses some degree of uniqueness, even if we are completely mediocre (unlikely!) in every other arena. There are some people, for example, who are remarkably compassionate and yet find it challenging to relate to their own families, while there are others who are fantastic in interfamily relationships, and are exemplary parents, children, brothers and sisters, but experience difficulties when working on a broader social level.

The areas of our brilliance in which we shine most brightly are directly related and correspond to our particular roots in the collective soul of Adam. Our conscious selves—our actions, words, thoughts, experiences and memories—become our personal soul for the span of our lives and for all eternity.

Our individuality, the spark of soul that fashioned our uniqueness (our soul inscription), does not—as a general principle—reincarnate, as it has already attained full *tikun.* Our *principium individuationis*—what makes us unique and guides us—requires no reincarnation.

What requires re-embodiment once our physical form is gone are the aspects of our soul with which we have had *little* experience.

The soul divides itself in the afterlife as it did during life. Just as in this earthly life there were sparks of soul with which we connected and others that remained dormant, this same phenomenon continues once consciousness separates from body. Sparks that were our soul in this life remain our soul for eternity, while other sparks reincarnate and gradually become individualized souls for other future bodies.

❧ *Life is a book and we are its authors*. Moment to moment we write and rewrite our own story. Every one of our stories is different, yet it is only by being totally true and open to our authentic selves, our unique *naran,* will our story reflect who we really are, and our spiritual uniqueness be actualized and expressed.

GATE 30

Gan Eden & Gehenom
Heaven & Hell

Every thought we entertain, every word spoken or deed perpetuated generates energy. This energy has a moral quality: positive thoughts, words and actions create positive energy, while negativity creates negative energy. Every action has a reaction, every cause has an effect. The principle of *sechar v'onesh*—reward and punishment—is folded within the context of *siba u'mesubav*—cause and effect.

While our thoughts, words and actions reflect our subjective reality, they also maintain an independent existence outside of ourselves. Our collective energies morph into an "objective correlative" to the subjective reality of who we are. As everything is seamlessly interwoven, everything we do has cosmic ripple effects, for now, and for the future.

The principle of cause and effect manifests internally through the traditional concept of: *sechar mitzvah, mitzvah*, the reward of a good deed, is the good deed itself. Positive thoughts, words and actions enlarge and open us to see the blessings in all of life, whereas negative thoughts, words or actions cut us off, alienate us, and throw us into a condition of restriction where everything in life seems like a curse.

We matter. Our actions matter. We can and do make a difference, for better or worse. There are personal and cosmic consequences to our actions. This truth is observable in our physical lives, and also extends into life beyond the physical.

The *naran* at birth is similar to a sheet of paper, colored with a particular shade but opened to be written upon by the author of life, which is each of us. We write our story and the story is life itself. Every experience we undergo, all the knowledge and wisdom we accumulate, is imprinted upon the fabric of our soul; our actions, words and thoughts become part of who we are.

The totality of each human being is present when personality disengages from body, at the moment of physical death. If the life story that we wrote is positive, eternal, noble and of value then our entire selves, all our entire memory will live on for eternity because positive actions are by their nature eternal. Memory of the individual within the Divine "memory" of the "everything" is *Gan Eden*—Paradise. In death as in life, the consciousness that remembers is also the content of what is remembered.

Gan Eden exists within the *sefira* of *binah*—divine intelligence. After a person's body passes, his or her memory will continue to flourish within the realm of *binah*. The *naran*, defined sense of self, which at birth contained the potential to survive after death in an active mode, continues to actualize based on what was achieved during life. In the world of the spirit there is constant movement and no room for complacency or dormancy.

Occasionally some of us accumulate much negativity during life. The negative is time/space bound, finite and restrictive and cannot continue to exist in eternity. Yet, because this negativity may be a part of us, we would need to go through a transitory process of ridding ourselves of negativity—this learning station is *Gehenom*—Hell.

When a soul is about to leave the body, the Zohar tells us, the *Shechinah* brilliantly appears and the soul goes out in joy and love to greet her. If during the soul's sojourn on earth the

person has become entrenched and immersed in material-
ism, to the extent of deriving its very sense of selfhood from
externals, the *Shechinah* drifts away and the soul is left alone
in mourning.

In other words, the Light of the *Shechinah* appears, and
instead of feeling the all embracing, comforting light of the
Shechinah, and the yearning to reconnect with one's Source, one
instead senses dread, panic, and an altogether overwhelming
feeling of fear. Instead of a heavenly experience, there is dread
and death becomes a hellish experience.

Fear is a by-product of the ego and its burning need for at-
tachments. Observing the light from an ego prism is fearful, as
one desperately clings to ego instead of surrendering lovingly
to the *Shechinah*. Tenaciously bounded with ego, a tension arises
with the realization of the transient nature of the ego and the
knowledge that it no longer serves a purpose. The need to give
it up provokes anguish, fear and uncertainty. This is hell.

A person who has lived a transcendent and noble life immediately senses the beauty of the experience and expires;
Others, who have not lived this way, retract, recoil and turn
aside; the presence of the *Shechinah* remains apart, and the soul
senses devastating emptiness.

For one who had lived a disharmonious existence, the light
of the *Shechinah* may be similar to sunlight absorbed without
the proper equipment; exquisite and picturesque but damaging
nonetheless. Light that is too intense blinds the observer and
becomes the source of darkness and confusion. *Gehenom* is the
absence of light, not because the Infinite Light is not present,
but because the light is too powerful to be appreciated by
spiritually estranged habitants. In due time these souls will
shine brightly, and the spiritual dirt that covers over their

essence will be shed.

❧ Throughout life we can either pick heaven or choose hell. Heaven is inclusive; hell is exclusive. In the heavenly paradigm it is me *and* you. In hell it is me *or* you. Heaven is an embracing condition of openness and transcendence; Hell is when every person we meet is suspected as an enemy, and every experience is threatening.

Hell is a state of total conflict with oneself, with other people, with our environment and with our Maker. Heaven, on the other hand, is harmonious co-existence with all levels of self, with other people, with all of creation and with our Creator. The choice is ours.

GATE 31

Ibbur & Dybbuk
Impregnation &
Attachments

As all souls are rooted within the "primordial soul of Adam": there are "head souls" and "hand souls," "heart souls," and "feet souls." Thus, all souls throughout history that are rooted in the "head of Adam" are intricately bound to one another, they are "soul relatives" as collectively they have a shared *tikun* to achieve.

Because they share a common overarching *tikun*, disembodied souls may come to be manifest within the presence of their "soul relative" to assist them in attaining their soul *tikun*. This is referred to as *ibbur*—impregnation. *Ibbur* is a guest soul that descends to assist, or to be assisted, by, the soul it inhabits.

Occasionally the following phenomenon may be attributed to *ibbur*: A person finds himself in a bad and negative space, where everything in life seems bleak and uncertain, and then one day when he wakes up, a tremendous shift has occurred, and he feels completely empowered, able and certain about his life.

A perfected soul may sense how a related soul is struggling to achieve its spiritual potential and therefore may re-descend to infuse that individual person with an extra dose of spiritual strength. Yet, in order for this extra dose of energy to be lasting, one needs to infuse inspiration from above with perspiration, hard work and effort from below. Otherwise

---

these experiences are pleasant, but of little lasting effect.

The opposite of positive *ibbur* is negative possession, *ruach ra*—bad spirit, also known as *dybbuk*—attached, cleaving as one.

Naked souls who are in a state of homelessness, neither in *Gan Eden*, paradise, nor in temporary residence of *Gehenom*, search out other locations to relocate and express themselves. These homeless souls may re-attach themselves to bodies on earth. Negative possession is perceived as an external alien invading force that is malevolent, hostile and disturbing. Most times, such feelings are mere chemical and psychological disorders that need to be dealt with medication not meditation, with physical treatment not spiritual therapy.

♣ If it is indeed an outside force that infringes upon our well being, whatever it may be, we can choose whether we merely surrender and become reactive, or take control and respond with mindfulness.

GATE 32

Guf Gas & Guf Dak
Coarse Body & Refined Body

As our *naran* is particularized and unique, with a distinct way of being, doing, feeling and thinking, the vehicle of our consciousness is also distinct. No two bodies are alike. On a physical level our *guf gas,* our physical bodies, have a particular formation. So, too, before our distinct *naran* becomes physically embodied there is a distinct garment to our soul, which is our *guf dak,* ethereal body. Before entering physical form, the Zohar writes, the soul hovers above in the very same form it will eventually embody.

We all posses both a *guf gas,* a dense body and a *guf dak,* an ethereal body. The *guf dak* is a spiritualized, luminous configuration that parallels our physical form, and serves as a medium to hold together consciousness and body.

Our relationship with our ethereal, angelic double is symbiotic and reciprocal. It is the conduit through which body expands and develops, and conversely it is also sustained and developed by our own projected thoughts and behaviors.

Everything we do, utter, think or feel generates energy. This energy field is positive or negative depending on the quality of our actions. When *naran* consciousness separates from the physical body at the moment of death, it first enters the ethereal body, and the nature of this afterlife body is a direct reflection of our actions, words, feeling and thoughts up until this moment.

Our collective energy field is also referred to as our *malbush* or *chulka,* garment, and also called our *tzelem* or *tzeil*—translated as shadow or aura. There is a spiritual phenomenon that is referred to as *hargashos ha'avir,* sensing the air, where one can sense another's aura, and on a deep level sense their soul, their thoughts, feelings and state of being.

❧ We all pick up signals. Since we all constantly project vibes into our immediate environment, when we radiate welcoming positive energy, the people to whom we are closest respond in kind, and the same is true for negativity. When we leak anger, for example, even when we don't speak of it, those around us pick it up and wish to stay away. Our faces and bodies constantly project our emotions, even those that we have not yet consciously registered.

Let's remember, everything we do has an effect, and ultimately we are only harming or benefiting ourselves by our actions. Let us chose wisely.

ABOUT THE AUTHOR

Rabbi Dov Ber is a scholar, author, thinker, and beloved spiritual teacher. Through his books and lectures, he has touched and inspired the lives of thousands. Amongst his published works are: *Reincarnation & Judaism: The Journey of the Soul*; *Inner Rhythms: The Kabbalah of Music*. *Meditation & Judaism: Exploring Meditative Paths*; *Toward the Infinite* and *Jewish Wisdom of the Afterlife*.

Rabbi Pinson is an internationally acclaimed speaker and has lectured in both scholarly and lay settings throughout the globe. Rabbi Pinson heads the IYYUN center in Brownstone Brooklyn. More information is available at Iyyun.com

CPSIA information can be obtained at www.ICGtesting.com
Printed in the USA
BVOW081132230613

323992BV00001B/3/P